በሚደብረኝ ጊዜ
When I Am Gloomy

ሳም ሳንልስኪ
ምስላዊ መግለጫ የተሠራው በዳኢያ ሲምስሎቫ

www.kidkiddos.com
Copyright ©2025 by KidKiddos Books Ltd.
support@kidkiddos.com

All rights reserved. No part of this book may be reproduced in any form or by any electronic or mechanical means, including information storage and retrieval systems, without written permission from the publisher, except in the case of a reviewer, who may quote brief passages embodied in critical articles or in a review.
First edition, 2025

Translated from English by Sosna Assefa
ከእንግሊዝኛ የተተረጎመው በሶስና አሰፋ

Library and Archives Canada Cataloguing in Publication
When I Am Gloomy (Amharic English Bilingual edition)/Shelley Admont
ISBN: 978-1-83416-789-3 paperback
ISBN: 978-1-83416-790-9 hardcover
ISBN: 978-1-83416-788-6 eBook

Please note that the Amharic and English versions of the story have been written to be as close as possible. However, in some cases they differ in order to accommodate nuances and fluidity of each language.

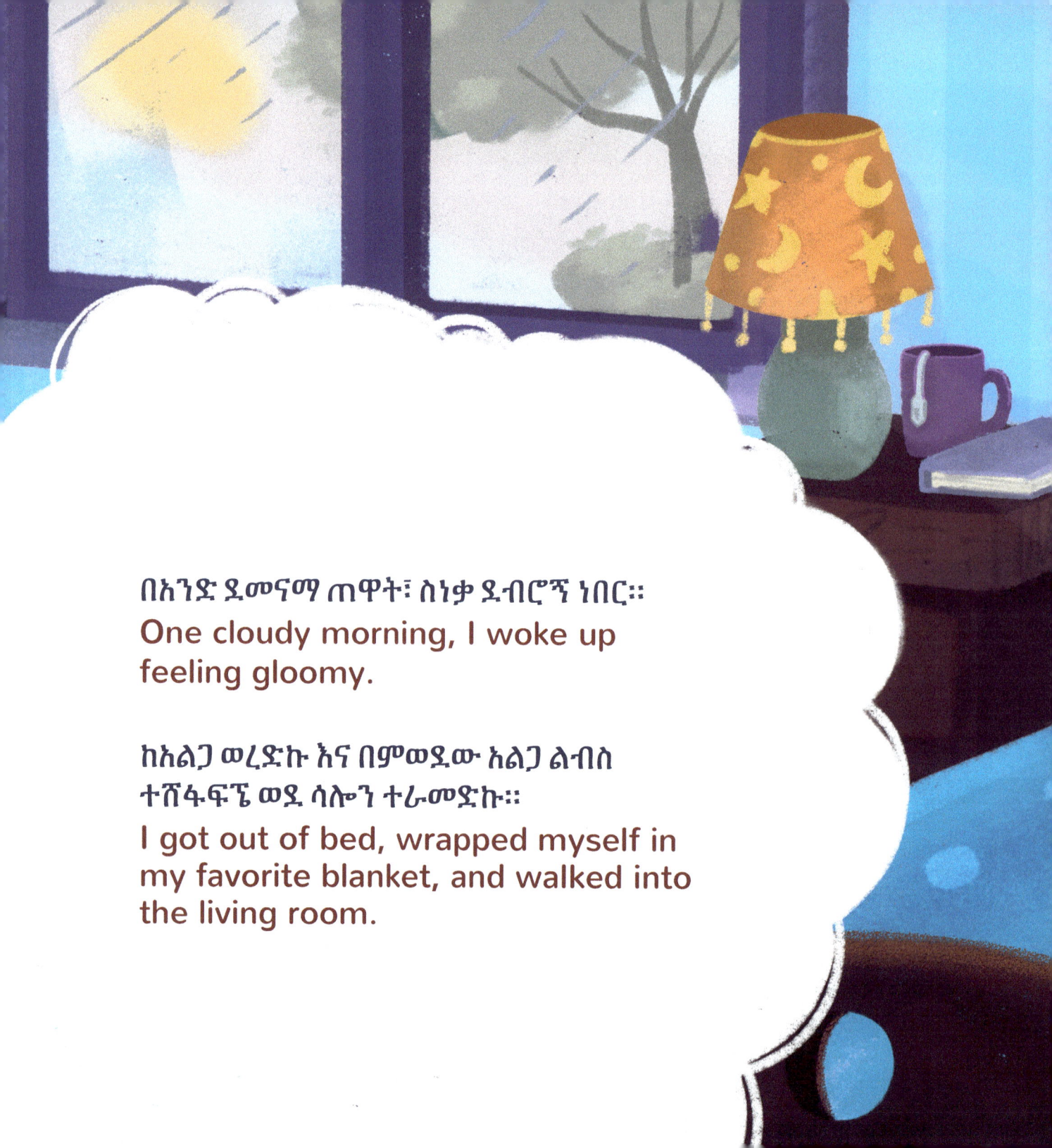

በአንድ ደመናማ ጠዋት፣ ስነቃ ደብሮኛ ነበር።
One cloudy morning, I woke up feeling gloomy.

ከአልጋ ወረድኩ እና በምወደው አልጋ ልብስ ተሸፋፍኜ ወደ ሳሎን ተራመድኩ።
I got out of bed, wrapped myself in my favorite blanket, and walked into the living room.

"እማዬ!" ብዬ ተጣራሁ። "ደብሮኛል።"
"Mommy!" I called. "I'm in a bad mood."

እማዬ ከያዘችው መጽሃፍ ቀና አለች። "ደብሮኛል? ለምን እንደዛ አልሽ የኔ ውድ?" በማለት ጠየቀችኝ።
Mom looked up from her book. "Bad? Why do you say that, darling?" she asked.

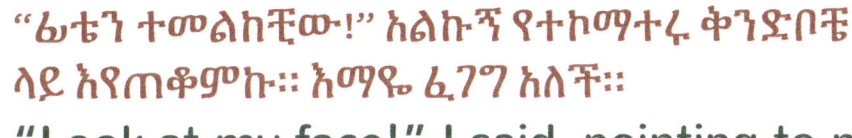

"ፊቴን ተመልከቺው!" አልኩኝ የተኮማተሩ ቅንድቦቼ ላይ እየጠቆምኩ። እማዬ ፈገግ አለች።
"Look at my face!" I said, pointing to my furrowed brows. Mom smiled gently.

"ዛሬ ፊቴ ደስተኛ አይደለም" በማለት አጉረመረምኩ። "በሚደብረኝ ጊዜ ትወጂኛለሽ?"
"I don't have a happy face today," I mumbled. "Do you still love me when I'm gloomy?"

"እዋ በትክክል" አለች እማዬ።
"በሚደብርሽ ጊዜ ለአንቺ ቅርብ መሆን፣ አንቺን ማቀፍ እና ማነቃቃት እፈልጋለሁ።"

"Of course I do," Mom said. "When you're gloomy, I want to be close to you, give you a big hug, and cheer you up."

ያ የተሻለ ስሜት እንዲሰማኝ አደረገ፣ ነገር ግን ለትንሽ ጊዜ ብቻ ነበር ምክንያቱም ስለሌሎች ስሜቶቼ ማሰብ ጀመርኩ።

That made me feel a little better, but only for a second, because then I started thinking about all my other moods.

"ስለዚህ... በምናደድ ጊዜም ትወጂኛለሽ?"
"So… do you still love me when I'm angry?"

እማዬ አሁንም ፈገግ አለች። "አዎ በትክክል!"
Mom smiled again. "Of course I do!"

"እርግጠኛ ነሽ?"
ብዬ ጠየቅኩ እጄን
አጣምሬ።
"Are you sure?"
I asked, crossing
my arms.

"በምትናደጂ ጊዜም እናትሽ ነኝ። እና በተመሳሳይ ሁኔታ እወድሻለሁ።"

"Even when you're mad, I'm still your mom. And I love you just the same."

ትልቅ ትንፋሽ ወሰድኩ።
"በማፍር ጊዜስ?" አልኩኝ
በመንሾካሾክ።
I took a big breath.
"What about when
I'm shy?" I whispered.

"በምታፍሪም ጊዜም እወድሻለሁ" አለች። "ከአዲሱ ጎረቤት ጋር ላለማውራት ከኋላዬ የተደበቅሽበት ቀን ትዝ ይልሻል?"
"I love you when you're shy too," she said. "Remember when you hid behind me and didn't want to talk to the new neighbor?"

ራሴን ነቀነኩ። በደንብ አስታውሼዋለሁ።
I nodded. I remembered it well.

"ከዚያ ሰላም አልሽ እና አዲስ ጓደኛ አፈራሽ። በጣም ኮርቼብሽ ነበር።"
"And then you said hello and made a new friend. I was so proud of you."

"በጣም ብዙ ጥያቄዎችን በምጠይቅ ጊዜም ትወጂኛለሽ?" በማለት ቀጠልኩ።

"Do you still love me when I ask too many questions?" I continued.

"ልክ እንደ አሁኑ ብዙ ጥያቄዎችን በምትጠይቂ ጊዜ፣ ጎበዝ እና ጠንካራ የሚያደርጉሽን አዳዲስ ነገሮች ስትማሪ ማየት እችላለሁ" አለች እማዬ። "እና አዎ፣ አሁንም እወድሻለሁ።"

"When you ask a lot of questions, like now, I get to watch you learn new things that make you smarter and stronger every day," Mom answered. "And yes, I still love you."

"ከነጭራሹ ማውራት ካልፈለኩስ?" በማለት ጥያቄዬን ቀጠልኩ።
"What if I don't feel like talking at all?" I continued asking.

"ነይ እስኪ" አለች። ጭኗ ላይ ተቀመጥኩ እና ጭንቅላቴን ትከሻዋ ላይ አሳረፍኩ።
"Come here," she said. I climbed into her lap and rested my head on her shoulder.

"ማውራት በማትፈልጊበት እና ዝም ማለት በምትፈልጊበት ጊዜ፣ ምናብሽን መጠቀም ትጀምሪያለሽ። የምትፈጥሪያቸውን ነገሮች መመልከት እወዳለሁ" አለች እማዬ።

"When you don't feel like talking and just want to be quiet, you start using your imagination. I love seeing what you create," Mom answered.

ከዚያ ወደ ጆሮዬ ተጠጋች እና በሹክሹክታ "ዝም ስትዪም እወድሻለሁ።" አለቺኝ።
Then she whispered in my ear, "I love you when you're quiet too."

"ግን በምፈራ ጊዜም ትወጂኛለሽ?" ብዬ ጠየቅኩ።
"But do you still love me when I'm afraid?" I asked.

"ሁሌም" አለች እማዬ። "በምትፈሪ ጊዜ፣ አልጋው ስር ወይም ቁም ሳጥን ውስጥ ጭራቅ እንደሌለ ለመፈተሽ አግዝሻለሁ።"
"Always," said Mom. "When you're scared, I help you check that there are no monsters under the bed or in the closet."

ግንባሬን ሳመችኝ። "በጣም ጀግና ነሽ፣ የኔ ጣፋጯ።"
She kissed me on the forehead. "You are so brave, my sweetheart."

"እና ደግሞ በሚደክምሽ ጊዜ" አለች ለስለስ ብላ፣ "በአልጋ ልብስ እሸፍንሽ እና አሻንጉሊትሽን አምጥቼ ልዩ መዝሙራችንን እዘምርልሻለሁ።"

"And when you're tired," she added softly, "I cover you with your blanket, bring you your teddy bear, and sing you our special song."

"ከመጠን በላይ ኃይል ቢኖረኛስ?" ብዬ ጠየቅኩ እየዘለልኩ።
"What if I have too much energy?" I asked, jumping to my feet.

ሳቀች። "ኃይልሽ ሙሉ ሲሆን፣ ብስክሌት ለመንዳት፣ ገመድ ለመዝለል ወይም ውጪ አብሮ ለመሮጥ እንወጣለን። እነዚያን ነገሮች በሙሉ ከአንቺ ጋር ማድረግ እወዳለሁ!"
She laughed. "When you're full of energy, we go biking, skip rope, or run around outside together. I love doing all those things with you!"

"ብሮኮሊ መብላት በማልፈልግ ጊዜ ግን ትወጂኛለሽ?" አልኩኝ ምላሴን አውጥቼ።

"But do you love me when I don't want to eat broccoli?" I stuck out my tongue.

እማዬ ሳቅ አለች። "ብሮኮሊሽን ለማክስ እንደሰጠሻው ጊዜ? እሱ ወዶት ነበር።"

Mom chuckled. "Like that time you slipped your broccoli to Max? He liked it a lot."

"አይተሽኛል?" ብዬ ጠየቅኩ።
"You saw that?" I asked.

"አዎ አይቼሻለሁ። እና ግን እንደዚያም ሆኖ እወድሻለሁ።"
"Of course I did. And I still love you, even then."

ለአፍታ አሰብኩ እና አንድ የመጨረሻ ጥያቄ ጠየቅኩ፡

I thought for a moment, then asked one last question:

"እማዬ፣ በሚደብረኝ ወይም በምናደድ ጊዜ የምትወጂኝ ከሆነ... ደስተኛ ስሆንም ትወጂኛለሽ?"

"Mommy, if you love me when I'm gloomy or mad… do you still love me when I'm happy?"

"ኦ የኔ ጣፋጭ" አለች እና በድጋሚ አቅፋኝ "ደስተኛ ስትሆኒ እኔም ደስተኛ ነኝ" አለች፡፡

"Oh, sweetheart," she said, hugging me again, "when you're happy, I'm happy too."

ግንባሬ ላይ ሳመችኝ እና "ደስተኛ ስትሆኒ ልክ በሚከፋሽ፣ በምትናደጂበት፣ በምታፍሪበት ወይም በሚደክምሽ ጊዜ እንደምወድሽ እወድሻለሁ፡፡" አለችኝ፡፡

She kissed me on the forehead and added, "I love you when you're happy just as much as I love you when you're sad, or mad, or shy, or tired."

ተጠጋኍት እና ፈገግ አልኩ። "ስለዚህ... ሁልጊዜ ትወጂኛለሽ? ብዬ ጠየቅኩ።

I snuggled close and smiled. "So… you love me all the time?" I asked.

"ሁልጊዜ" አለች። "በሁሉም አይነት ስሜት፣ በየዕለቱ፣ ሁሌም እወድሻለሁ።"

"All the time," she said. "Every mood, every day, I love you always."

በምትናገርበት ጊዜ ልቤ ውስጥ ሙቀት ተሰማኝ፡፡

As she spoke, I started feeling something warm in my heart.

ወደ ውጪ ተመለከትኩ እና ደመናዎቹ ሲንሳፈፉ አየሁ፡፡ ሰማዩ ሰማያዊ ሆነ እና ጸሃይ ወጣች፡፡

I looked outside and saw the clouds floating away. The sky was turning blue, and the sun came out.

ቆንጆ ቀን የሚሆን ይመስላል፡፡

It looked like it was going to be a beautiful day after all.

www.ingramcontent.com/pod-product-compliance
Lightning Source LLC
LaVergne TN
LVHW072008060526
838200LV00010B/295